Diet recommendations for TCM - Lung - Qi deficiency

Please check these recommendations always with a TCM nutrition consultant, therapist, doctor or dietician. The recipes and the list of ingredients are supporting also the conventional medical therapy. The calorie disclosures of fresh ingredients (fruit and vegetables) vary according to quality and time of harvest. The contents were checked by a dietician and a nutrition consultant for the Traditional Chinese Medicine (TCM).

Author:
©2017 Josef Miligui
www.ebns.at

AF285237

Source:
The lists are created from the EBNS database for nutritional counseling. The database is used by dietitians, therapists and doctors for advising the patient / client.

Literature:
The specialist literature and the training documents of the German and Austrian dietary and traditional Chinese medicine serve as a knowledge base. We have used the documents as a basis of knowledge, adapted it to our experience and completed them.
http://di-book.com

Title Photo:
©2008 Erika Weixlbaumer

Production and publishing:
BoD – Books on Demand, Norderstedt
ISBN: 9783752862362

Diet recommendations for TCM - Lung - Qi deficiency

1   Treatment strategy

Build up lung qi, strengthen center, strengthen kidney.
Hot LITTLE, warm and neutral YES, refreshing LITTLE, cold NO

2   Avoid

Everything that weakens spleen, sugar, denatured (frozen food),
tropical fruits and raw foods, yogurt, ice cream, cold foods or drinks,
dairy products, black tea, coffee, factory sugar.

3   Breakfast

	kkal. per serving
Beef broth	124
Chickpeas with Raisins	429
Coconut rice with cardamom	266
Compote of pears	122
Leek soup with almondmash	115
Millet mash with steamed pears	235
Millet with egg and butter	338
Pear compote	100
Pear juice	180
Reissue soup with fresh fruits	143
Rice congee with carrots and fennel	131
Rice congee with crushed walnuts	406
Rice congee with dried fruit	210
Rice congee with honey pear and black sesame	158
Rice dulse soup	190
Rice noodle soup with shiitake mushrooms	65
Roasted oatmeal with grapes compote	328

4 Snack

5 Lunch

6   Afternoon

7   Dinner

8   Any time

9 Recipes

(recommendable) = You can use more.
(little) = You should use less than specified or omit.

9.1 8 treasures of rice

Strengthens kidney and bladder, builds up Qi, strengthens the spleen, repels moisture, reduces internal heat, prevents cancer, builds heart, calms nerves.
Cooking time approx. 1 hour
 Calories p. portion: 212
4 portions

Quantity of ingredients
Lily bulbs 1 table spoon / 5g. (recommended).................................. *
Longane 1 table spoon / 5g. (little)... *
King Solomon's-seal 1 table spoon / 5g. (recommended)................. *
Yam root, yam root tuber 1 table spoon / 5g. (recommended)........... *
Coix (seeds) YiYi Ren 1 table spoon / 5g. (little) .... *
Rice wild (nature rice) 1 1/2 cups / 240g. (yes) .... metal
Water 8-10 cups / 800g. (yes) .... earth

Cooking instructions:
Each one 1 tbsp: Bai He, Longan, Yu Zhu, Da Zao, Shan Yao, Lian Mi, Yi Yi Ren, Qian Shi
Add hot water and soak for about 30 minutes. Then add 1 - 2 cups of rice (normal) and simmer for 1/2 to 1 hour until the rice is very soft. Or: Cook for about 3 hours with the herbs a congee. Then the herbs do not have to be soaked.

9.2 Basic recipe for a beef broth (clear)

Strengthens Qi and Yang, is very warming.
Cooking time approx. 4-8 hours
Calories p. portion: 114
10 portions
Allergens: O

Quantity of ingredients
Beef soup meat 1,1 lbs / 500g. .... earth
Beef meatbones 5/8 oz / 200g. .... earth
Vinegar (Red wine vinegar) 1 dash / 3g. .... wood

Juniper berry 8 pieces / 6g. .... fire
Rosemary 1 pinch / 1g. .... fire
Carrot 3 pieces / 210g. .... earth
Parsnip 2 pieces / 300g. .... fire
Leek 1 piece / 200g. ....metal
Ginger fresh 1/2 teaspoon / 5g. ....metal
Lovage 1 stem / 15g. ....metal
Clove 2 pieces / 2g. ....metal
Pimento 6 pieces / 12g. ....metal
Anise (Common Fennel) 2 pieces / 1g. .... earth
Salt 1 teaspoon / 5g. ....water
Water 3,3 lbs / 1300g. .... earth

Cooking instructions:
Heat water, a dash of red wine vinegar, some juniper berries, a little
rosemary, bones and meat till it boils; add carrot, parsnip, leek, ginger,
lovage, clove, allspice, star anise and a little salt; simmer for 4-8 hours
then strain.
Refrigerate for later use.

9.3   Basic recipe for a chicken broth worming

Strengthens Qi and blood, is very warm.
Cooking time approx. 2-3 hours
Calories p. portion: 90
9 portions
Allergens: L

Quantity of ingredients
Chicken meat 1/2 piece / 600g. ....wood
Carrot 2 pieces / 150g. .... earth
Leek 1 stick / 45g. ....metal
Celery root 1 piece / 500g. .... earth
Ginger fresh 2 slices / 2g. ....metal
Fenugreek (Trigonella foenum-graecum) 1 teaspoon / 2g. ....*
Juniper berry 1 teaspoon / 3g. .... fire
Bay leaf 3 pieces / 2g. ....*
Water 4 cup / 900g. .... earth

Cooking instructions:
Remove chicken parts from fat. Place chicken pieces in a saucepan with hot water and heat till it boils briefly, skimming any resulting foam. Add coarsely chopped vegetables and all spices and cook over medium heat for 2 to 3 hours. Strain the finished soup. Throw away vegetables and bones.
Tip: If you want to use the meat as a soup insert, take out after 45 minutes and return only the bones in the soup.
Refrigerate for later use.

9.4   Basic recipe for a reissue soup (Congee)

Warms the stomach and spleen, harmonizes the intestine, forces Qi, reduces moisture.
Cooking time approx. 2-4 hours
Calories p. portion: 140
3 portions
Allergens:

Quantity of ingredients
Rice variety any 1 cup / 120g. ....metal
Water 6 cups / 700g. .... earth

Cooking instructions:
Cook rice and water in a ratio of about 1: 6. The amount of water determines the thickness of the mash (matter of taste).
Put the rice in a saucepan with a heavy lid. It is important to simmer the rice after a short boil on the slightest flame, otherwise it burns.
Boil the rice for 2-4 hours. The longer he cooks, the more he strengthens.
If you want to eat the dish for breakfast, you can put the rice on just before bedtime.
To be on the safe side, you should first check the behavior of your pot and cooker under observation for a similar amount of time, so that nothing burns.
Refrigerate for later use.

9.5 Basic recipe for a vegetable soup, nutritious

Strengthens spleen and lung, regulates Qi flow, builds up Qi, dries out, passes downwardly, strengthens stomach Qi.
Cooking time approx. 2-3 hours
Calories p. portion: 48
5 portions
Allergens: L

Quantity of ingredients

Olive oil 1 table spoon / 4g. .... earth
Onion white 1 piece / 60g. ....metal
Carrot 3 pieces / 200g. .... earth
Parsnip 3/8 lbs - 6oz / 150g. .... fire
Celery root 1 cup / 100g. .... earth
Ginger fresh 1/2 teaspoon / 2g. ....metal
Lemon 1/2 piece / 25g. .... wood
Juniper berry 6 pieces / 6g. .... fire
Thyme dried 1 pinch / 1g. ....metal
Lovage 1 table spoon / 3g. ....metal
Bay leaf 2 leaves / 1g. .... *
Salt 1 pinch / 1g. ....water
Water 3 cups / 650g. .... earth

Cooking instructions:

Cut the vegetables into cubes.
Heat oil in hot pot, fry shortly onions and vegetables.
Add cold water, then add ginger, bay leaf and lemon juice.
Season with juniper, thyme and lovage. Cover for 2 - 3 hours on a low heat and simmer.
The used vegetables should be thrown away.
The basic recipe serves as a soup base and to refine vegetables, legumes or cereals.
If you want to eat vegetable soup immediately, add the desired vegetables half an hour before.
Refrigerate for later use.

9.6 Beef broth

Warming and nourishing, builds up Qi, strengthens blood and fluids.
Cooking time approx. 2-6 hours
Calories p. portion: 125
7 portions
Allergens: L

Quantity of ingredients
Water 4 cup / 1000g. (yes) .... earth
Lemon 2 dashes / 2g. .... wood
Beef meat 1,1 lbs / 500g. (yes) .... earth
Beef meatbones 2 pieces / 0g. (yes) .... earth
Turmeric (yellow root) 1 pinch / 1g. (recommended) .... *
Carrot 2 pieces / 100g. (recommended) .... earth
Celery root 1 inch / 25g. (recommended) .... earth
Parsley root 1 piece / 150g. (recommended) .... earth
Onion white 1 piece / 50g. (yes) .... metal
Bay leaf 2-3 leaves / 2g. (recommended) .... *
Coriander 1/2 teaspoon / 2g. (recommended) .... metal
Ginger fresh 1 inch / 2g. (recommended) .... metal
Wakame 1 inch / 1g. (little) .... water
Parsley 1 stem / 10g. (recommended) .... wood

Cooking instructions:
In a saucepan with water (enough to cover the meat), add a few drops
of lemon juice, a little turmeric, beef and bones, heat till it boils and
simmer for a while; then pour away the whole broth, clean the pot, rinse
off meat and bones with hot water (this will save you from foaming) and
put it back to the saucepan with hot water (amount as you like); add a
good pinch of turmeric, carrot, celery, parsley root to the pot; add onion,
bay leaves, coriander, a piece of sliced ginger, a strip of wakame, a
stalk of parsley; boil everything together and simmer for 2-6 hours (if the
meat is to be used otherwise, take it out of the broth after 1 1/2 - 2
hours, as soon as it is cooked, the bones are returned to the broth);
When the cooking time is over, pour the broth through a sieve and
discard all ingredients.

Notes: The longer the broth has cooked, the warmer but more
nourishing it is. It is after cooling for 3-4 days in the refrigerator durable.
The broth can be drunk hot or used as a base for soups with cereals,
potatoes and fresh vegetables.

9.7 Beef soup with carrots, leeks, bay leaves

Strengthens spleen Qi, strengthens blood and Qi, moisturizes, relaxes, builds up Qi, spreads, strengthens spleen and liver, regulates Qi flow, strengthens stomach Qi.
Cooking time approx. 2-3 hours
Calories p. portion: 194
5 portions

Quantity of ingredients
Beef meat 1 lbs / 500g. (yes).. earth
Carrot 2 pieces / 200g. (recommended).................................... earth
Leek 1/2 piece / 150g. (recommended) ....metal
Bay leaf 3 leaves / 1g. (recommended) .... *
Corn Grease (Polenta) 1 table spoon / 10g. (little) .... earth
Water 2 cup / 450g. (yes).. earth
Salt 1 pinch / 0,5g. (recommended)...water

Cooking instructions:
In a saucepan with water (enough to cover the meat), add beef soup meat or leg slice and simmer for a moment; then pour off the broth, rinse the meat with hot water (this will save you from foaming), clean the pot and put the meat in hot water again; add chopped carrot, leek, corn and bay leaf; simmer until the meat is cooked.

9.8 Beluga lentil stew with vegetables

Tonifies Qi and blood, forces kidneys and spleen, dissipates heat and moisture.
Cooking time approx. 20 min
Calories p. portion: 201
5 portions

Quantity of ingredients
Lentils 1 1/2 cups / 240g. (recommended) ....water
Water 4-5 cups / 500g. (yes) .... earth
Carrot 3 pieces / 150g. (recommended).................................... earth
Leek 1 piece / 300g. (recommended) ....metal
Kohlrabi 1/2 piece / 200g. (recommended) .... earth
Tomato 2 pieces / 80g. ....wood
Onion white 1 piece / 50g. (yes) ....metal
Bay leaf 2 leaves / 1g. (recommended) .... *
Fennel 1 piece / 250g. (recommended) .... earth
Star anise 2 pieces / 1g. (yes).. *

Juniper berry 6 pieces / 2g. (little)... fire
Olive oil 2 table spoons / 30g. (little) .... earth
Salt 1 pinch / 1g. (recommended)...water
Ginger fresh 1/2 teaspoon / 2g. (recommended).......................metal
Black caraway 1 pinch / 1g. (recommended) .... *

Cooking instructions:
Heat oil in hot pot. Fry onions and add diced vegetables and spices,
lentils (washed well) and salt. Cover with cold water (3 fingers wide)
and cook for 20 minutes on a low heat.
Sprinkle with fresh herbs and black cumin

Goes well with rice!

9.9   Black-eyed beans stew

Strengthens spleen and kidney, is very nutritious, warms the stomach
and spleen, harmonizes the intestine, forces Qi, strengthens stomach
and kidney, strengthens spleen and kidney.
Cooking time approx. 20 min
Calories p. portion: 140
5 portions

Quantity of ingredients
Black-eyed peas 1 cup / 100g. (recommended)..........................water
Rice variety any 1 1/2 cups / 200g. (yes) ....metal
Water 10 cups / 1000g. (yes)... earth

Cooking instructions:
Soak the beans overnight and strain.

In a ratio of 1: 2, simmer the beans together with the rice in the Water.
Depending on how hot the flame is and how thin the dish should be,
more water must be added.

Variation: Add vegetables fried in oil, such as carrots, celery tubers,
onions or leeks.

9.10 Boiled fillet with potatoebiscuits (Austrian Tafelspitz)

Strengthens spleen Qi, strengthens blood and Qi, moisturizes, relaxes, builds up Qi, spreads, forces Qi, forces spleen, relieves inflammation.
Cooking time approx. 3 hours
Calories p. portion: 454
8 portions
Allergens: L

Quantity of ingredients
Onion white 1 piece / 50g. (yes) ....metal
Corn germ oil 1 table spoon / 10g. (recommended) .... earth
Water 32 cup - 1 gallon / 0g. (yes).. earth
Beef meat 5,4 lbs - 70oz cap of rump / 1800g. (yes).................. earth
Beef meatbones 4n slices with bone marrow / 0g. (yes)............. earth
Salt 1 pinch / 0,5g. (recommended)...water
Peppercorns 15 pieces / 0g. (yes) ....metal
Parsnip 1 piece / 0g. (recommended)... fire
Carrot 2 pieces / 0g. (recommended) .... earth
Celery root 1 slice / 0g. (recommended) .... earth
Parsley root 2 pieces / 0g. (recommended).................................. earth
Leek 1/2 stick / 0g. (recommended)..metal
Chives 1 table spoon (chopped) / 7g. (recommended)...............metal
Potato 2,2 lbs / 1000g. (recommended)...................................... earth
Sunflower oil 2 table spoons / 20g. (recommended)................... earth
Salt 1 pinch / 0,5g. (recommended)...water

Cooking instructions:
Halve the onions, but do not peel. Brown onions in a pan with fat on the cut surfaces very dark. Wash meat and bones briefly with warm water, drain.
Heat the water till it boils, put in meat and cook gently. Always scoop up rising foam. As soon as no more foam rises, add peppercorns and the onion. Clean and cut root and leeks and add after about two and a half hours cooking time. Simmer for another half hour.
Remove boiled beef from the soup, pour through a sieve and season with salt. Cut roots into bite-sized pieces. Add the soup together with the marrow bones and leave it under the boiling point. Cut the boiled beef into finger-thick slices against the grain, place in the soup, heat again, sprinkle with a little chives. In addition, cook and peel the potatoes in salted water. Stomp roughly or cut finely. Fry in a pan with the oil crispy.

9.11 Carp soup

Nourishing and slightly warming, strengthens the middle and the lower heater, removes moisture.
Cooking time approx. 2 hours
Calories p. portion: 499
2 portions
Allergens: DO

Quantity of ingredients
Carp 1,1 lbs / 500g. (recommended) ....water
Salt 1 pinch / 1g. (recommended)...water
Vinegar (Apple vinegar) 1 teaspoon / 3g. (little) ....wood
Thyme 1 Twig / 3g. (recommended) ....*
Juniper berry 8 pieces / 3g. (little)... fire
Carrot 2 pieces / 200g. (recommended)..................................... earth
Leek 1 piece / 200g. (recommended) ....metal
Onion white 1 piece / 60g. (yes) ....metal
Ginger fresh 1/2 teaspoon / 2g. (recommended).......................metal
Bay leaf 3 leaves / 1g. (recommended) ....*
White wine 1/2 cup / 125g. (little)..wood
Basil 3 leaves / 1g. (recommended)...metal

Cooking instructions:
Preparation: When shopping at the fishmonger, remove the fillets from a medium-sized, whole carp and also pack the fish head, spine with bones and tail.

Cut the fillets into 1 cm cubes; salt and set aside.

Place fish head, backbone and tail of carp in plenty of cold water; heat till it boils and scoop the foam; add a dash of vinegar, a fresh sprig of thyme, juniper berries; Add carrot, a piece of leek and chopped onion; add a thick slice of ginger, some peppercorns, 1 bay leaf, salt; simmer for about 1 1/2 hours and pour the stock through a sieve.

Put the carp pieces in a saucepan; pour a shot of white wine; Add rose paprika, basil leaves, finely ground carrots, dried thyme and the stock and warm; Boil the ingredients for about 5 minutes until the fish pieces are cooked.
Variants: Thicken the soup with kudzu or mashed potatoes.
This fits: baguette and dry white wine.

9.12 Chicken soup with angelica root and buckthorn fruit

Strengthens spleen and nourishes the blood and Yin of the liver, forces Qi and blood, is very warming.
Cooking time approx. 1 1/2 hours
Calories p. portion: 77
3 portions
Allergens: LO

Quantity of ingredients
Basic recipe for a chicken soup 2 cup / 500g. (recommended) .... *
Angelica root 1/8 oz / 5g. (recommended) .... *
Bocksdorn fruits, goji berry dried 1/8 lbs - 2oz / 50g. .... wood

Cooking instructions:
When you cook chicken broth according to basic recipes add angelica root and Bocksdorn fruits in the last 40 minutes.

Ingestion: Drink 2-3 cups of broth daily.

9.13 Chickpeas with Raisins

Strengthens spleen and liver, regulates Qi flow, moisturizes, relaxes, builds up Qi, spreads, strengthens spleen and heart, softens, passes downwardly, warms the stomach and spleen, harmonizes the intestine, forces Qi, reduces moisture.
Cooking time approx. 45 min
Calories p. portion: 429
2 portions
Allergens: EGO

Quantity of ingredients
Chickpeas 1 cup / 120g. (recommended) .... water
Hijiki 1 table spoon / 7g. (recommended)................................... water
Salt 1 pinch / 0,5g. (recommended).. water
Sunflower oil 1 table spoon / 10g. (recommended) .... earth
Carrot 2 pieces / 160g. (recommended).................................... earth
Raisins 2 table spoons / 18g. (yes).. earth
Ginger fresh 1/2 teaspoon / 2g. (recommended)....................... metal

Cumin (Caraway seed) 1 pinch / 0,2g. (yes)...............................metal
Lemon juice 1 dash / 1g. ....wood
Sour cream 15% fat 1 table spoon / 8g. ....*
Curcuma 1 pinch / 0,2g. (little)...*
Soybean milk 1 dash / 1g. (little).. earth
Coriander 1 pinch / 0,2g. (recommended)..................................metal
Soy sauce 1 dash / 1g. ....water
Rice round grain 1/2 cup / 60g. (recommended).......................metal
Water 3 cups / 250g. (yes) .... earth
Salt 1 pinch / 1g. (recommended)..water

Cooking instructions:
Preparation:
Soak chickpeas in cold water for several hours or overnight.

After that:
Pour soaking water away; put the chickpeas in cold water; Add 1 tbsp Hijiki and cook the chickpeas bite-proof; Add salt at the end of the cooking time.

Separately:
In a hot pan, fry oil, chopped carrots (more than chickpeas), raisins, grated ginger, plenty of cumin and salt until the carrots are half cooked; add the chickpeas and sea algae; Add lemon juice, a little sour cream, turmeric, soy or rice milk; a pinch of cilantro, add some soy sauce; Let it soak for a few minutes over low heat until the carrots are cooked.

Put the round grain rice with the water, salt and cook for about 20 minutes.

9.14 Classic ginger chicken with rice wine

warming and nourishing, directs the Qi upwards, forces the libido, against Qi- und Yang-weakness of spleen, heart and kidneys, in lung Qi deficiency, moisture, sensitivity to cold, listlessness.
Cooking time approx. 30 min
Calories p. portion: 357
4 portions
Allergens: GO

Quantity of ingredients

Butter organic 2 table spoons / 30g. (recommended)................. earth
Ginger fresh 2 table spoons / 18g. (recommended) .... metal
Salt 1 pinch / 0,5g. (recommended)... water
Chicken meat 2 pieces (legs) / 500g. (recommended) .... wood
Lychee liqueur 1 dash / 2g. (recommended)................................. fire
Curry 1 pinch / 1g. .... metal
Sake 1 dash / 1g. (recommended)... metal
Corn 4 table spoons / 30g. (little).. earth
Millet 1/2 cup / 50g. (little)... earth
Water 1 1/2 cups / 200g. (yes).. earth
Salt 1 pinch / 0,1g. (recommended).. water
Lettuce 1/2 piece / 100g. .... fire
Olive oil 1 table spoon / 10g. (little).. earth
Vinegar (Apple vinegar) 1 teaspoon / 3g. (little) .... wood
Water 2 table spoons / 20g. (yes)... earth
Salt 1 pinch / 0,5g. (recommended).. water
Herbs various 1 table spoon / 8g. (recommended)............................ *

Cooking instructions:

Heat butter in a hot pan (preferably made of cast iron or enamel); sauté chopped ginger (about 1 heaped tablespoons per chicken leg) on low heat; add some salt, chicken and/or other parts of the chicken and roast all around with gentle heat; add Lychee liqueur or maple syrup, add a little curry and fry for a short time; stir in plenty of sake; add corn kernels (from the glass, health food trade); boil all the ingredients in the sauce for a few minutes, until the meat is cooked; season with salt.

This fits: millet, lettuce or lettuce.

9.15 Clear oxen tail soup with buckthorn fruit

Forces Qi, nourishes the liver blood, good for ocular fibrillation or dry eyes, muscle tension or calf cramps due to blood deficiency.
Cooking time approx. 1-2 hours
Calories p. portion: 217
6 portions
Allergens: O

Quantity of ingredients

Basic recipe for a beef soup 4 cup / 1000g. (recommended)..............*
Beef Oxtail pieces 1,1 lbs / 500g. (recommended)..................... earth
Shiitake, dried 4-5 pieces / 4g. (recommended)......................... earth
Onion white 1 piece / 60g. (yes) ....metal
Sake 2 table spoons / 20g. (recommended)..............................metal
Ginger fresh 1/2 teaspoon / 2g. (recommended)........................metal
Bocksdorn fruits, goji berry dried 1 table spoon / 8g. .... wood

Cooking instructions:

Soak shiitake mushrooms. Blanch oxtail slices (This removes fat and impurities).
Cook in the beef broth for 1-2 hours.
Then add the spring onions, shiitake mushrooms, rice wine, buckthorn fruits and ginger and simmer gently.

9.16 Clear soup from goose

Forces spleen, stomach and lungs, relieves weakness, forces Qi, calms the stomach, gets Qi moving, directs upwards, strengthens spleen and liver, regulates Qi flow, moisturizes, relaxes, builds up Qi, spreads.
Cooking time approx. 2-3 hours
Calories p. portion: 334
6 portions

Quantity of ingredients

Goose parts 1,1 lbs / 500g. (recommended)..............................metal
Carrot 1 piece / 100g. (recommended) .... earth
Onion (shallot) 1 piece / 25g. (yes)...metal
Leek 1 piece / 250g. (recommended) ....metal
Parsley 1 Twig / 4g. (recommended) .... wood
Lovage 1 Twig / 4g. (recommended) ....metal
Chervil 1 pinch / 0,2g. (recommended) ....*
Water 4 cup / 1000g. (yes) .... earth
Salt 1 pinch / 0,5g. (recommended)..water

Cooking instructions:

Simmer goose pieces with vegetables and herbs for 2-3 hours. Sift through a fine cloth and cool. Degrease and store in the refrigerator.

9.17 Coconut rice with cardamom

Forces lungs and spleen, diuretic, forces Qi, protects liver, forces stomach and spleen, forces muscles, reduces moisture, strengthens Qi and Kidney Jing, strengthens Qi of the heart and lungs, quenches thirst.
Cooking time approx. 45 min
Calories p. portion: 266
4 portions
Allergens: GO

Quantity of ingredients
Rice long grain rice 1 cup / 120g. (yes).....................................metal
Water 6 cups / 400g. (yes) .... earth
Sugar cane sugar 1 table spoon / 10g. (little)............................. earth
Cardamom 1 teaspoon / 2g. (recommended)....................................*
Ginger fresh 1/2 teaspoon / 2g. (recommended).........................metal
Butter organic 2 table spoons / 20g. (recommended)................. earth
Coconut grated 2 table spoons / 16g. (little).............................. earth
Cashews 1 table spoon / 8g. (little)... earth
Raisins 1 table spoon / 8g. (yes)... earth
Salt 1 pinch / 0,5g. (recommended)...water
Lemon 1/2 piece / 15g. .... wood
Pumpkin 3/4 lbs / 300g. (recommended) .... earth
Olive oil 2 table spoons / 20g. (little).. earth
Coriander 1 pinch / 0,2g. (recommended)..................................metal
Pepper (ground) 1 pinch / 0,2g. (yes) ....metal
Curry 1 pinch / 0,5g. ....metal
Water 1/4 cup / 50g. (yes) .... earth
Salt 1 pinch / 0,5g. (recommended)...water
Parsley 1 table spoon / 8g. (recommended)............................... wood
Cardamom 1 pinch / 0,2g. (recommended)......................................*
Turmeric (yellow root) 1 pinch / 0,2g. (recommended) ....*

Cooking instructions:
Preparation: Soak long grain rice in cold water for 1 hour and drain.
Then: Heat fresh water till it boils; add some whole cane sugar, plenty of ground cardamom or some cardamom pods, grated ginger and the rice into the hot water and cook.
Separately: heat some butter in a hot pot; add grated coconut, cashews and raisins; add the cooked rice and salt; pour lemon juice over it; mix everything and let it pass for a few minutes.
Pumpkin vegetables: heat olive oil in a pan. Steam the pumpkin (cut in cubes), season with cilantro, pepper and curry, simmer with a little

water, salt with sea salt, add chopped parsley with cardamom and turmeric, simmer on a small fire for about 10 minutes, depending on the pumpkin, the pumpkin should still be firm.

9.18 Compote of pears

Forces lung Qi. Ideal as a cure in the fall.
Cooking time approx. 10 min
Calories p. portion: 122
4 portions

Quantity of ingredients
Water 1 cup / 280g. (yes) .... earth
Pear 4 pieces / 800g. (recommended) .... earth
Anise (Common Fennel) 1/2 teaspoon / 1g. (yes) .... earth
Vanilla pod 1 pinch / 1g. (recommended) .... *
Cocoa 1 pinch / 1g. (little) .... fire

Cooking instructions:
Boil pears (organic - with peel), aniseed, vanilla, chili soft. Sprinkle with cocoa.

9.19 Fennel and potato gratin

Regulates Qi, warms the inside, lowers cold, forces stomach, relieves constipation, forces Yang, dissolves mucus, reduces wind, spreads. forces Qi, forces spleen, relaxes, builds up Qi, spreads.
Cooking time approx. 1 1/2 hours
Calories p. portion: 147
2 portions
Allergens: CGL

Quantity of ingredients
Fennel 5/8 oz / 200g. (recommended) .... earth
Potato 1/4 lbs - 4oz / 125g. (recommended) .... earth
Basic recipe for a vegetable soup (nutritious) 1/2 cup / 100g. (recommended)*
Butter organic 1 teaspoon / 3g. (recommended) .... earth
Rice flour 2 teaspoons / 6g. (yes) .... metal
Cream sour 10% 1 teaspoon / 3g. (recommended) .... *
Salt 1 pinch / 1g. (recommended) .... water
Sugar cane sugar 1 pinch / 1g. (little) .... earth
Chicken yolk 1 piece / 10g. (recommended) .... earth
Pepper Cayenne 1 pinch / 0,5g. (yes) .... metal

Nutmeg 1 pinch / 0,5g. (little)..metal
Parsley 1 teaspoon / 2g. (recommended) ....wood
Chives 1 teaspoon / 3g. (recommended) ....metal
Parmesan 1 teaspoon / 3g. .... earth
Butter organic 1 teaspoon / 3g. (recommended) .... earth

Cooking instructions:
Cook peeled potatoes and then let cool. Wash the fennel, cut off the stems and remove any outer leaves.
Hold back fennel greens and add it to the sauce with the other herbs later.
Steam the fennel tubers for about 15 - 20 minutes.
Then cut the potatoes and fennel into slices and place in layers in a greased baking dish.
Bring the liquid of fennel broth to the boil and bind it with flour.
Season with sea salt, cayenne pepper, sugar, nutmeg and sour cream. Allow to cool and alloy with egg yolk.
Spread the sauce over the casserole, sprinkle with parmesan and finely chopped parsley and chives. Bake at 200 °C / 392 °F in the oven for half an hour.

9.20 Indian Dal soup

Reduces internal heat and moisture, softens, passes downwardly, strengthens spleen and liver, regulates Qi flow, moisturizes, relaxes, builds up Qi, spreads, forces liver and kidney, reduces damp heat.
Cooking time approx. 30 min
Calories p. portion: 256
2 portions
Allergens: EN

Quantity of ingredients
Lentils 3/8 lbs - 6oz / 175g. (recommended) ....water
Sesame oil 2 table spoons / 30g. (recommended) .... earth
Carrot 1 piece / 100g. (recommended) .... earth
Onion (shallot) 1 piece / 15g. (yes)...metal
Water 1 1/2 cups / 200g. (yes)... earth
Ginger fresh 2 slices / 1g. (recommended) ....metal
Salt 1 pinch / 0,5g. (recommended)...water
Soy sauce 1 teaspoon / 3g. ....water
Parsley 1 teaspoon (chopped) / 3g. (recommended).................. wood
Thyme 1 teaspoon / 3g. (recommended) .... *
Basil 1 table spoon / 5g. (recommended)...................................metal

Cooking instructions:
Soak the lentils overnight.
in a hot pot, carrot, onion and a little ginger fry, pour water. Add the lentils and cook until soft. Add salt or soy sauce and cook for another 10 minutes.
Stir in parsley before serving; Sprinkle thyme or basil over it.
Variant: Other herbs such as sage, rosemary or lovage allow a variety of flavors.

9.21 Japanese algae soup

Strengthens spleen and liver, regulates Qi flow, moisturizes, relaxes, builds up Qi, spreads, nourishes the lungs and spleen, distributes mucus, dissolves mucus, dissolves stagnation, directs upwards, gets Qi moving und Yang.
Cooking time approx. 20 min
Calories p. portion: 47
3 portions

Quantity of ingredients
Wakame 1 oz / 25g. (little)..water
Water 2 cup / 450g. (yes).. earth
Onion (shallot) 1-2 pcs. / 30g. (yes)...metal
Radish (white, green, purple-red) 1/8 lbs - 2oz / 50g. (yes)........metal
Carrot 2 pieces / 180g. (recommended)..................................... earth
Miso 2 table spoons / 20g. (recommended) ....water
Parsley 2 table spoons / 20g. (recommended)...........................wood
Onion (spring onion) 1 table spoon (sliced)................................metal

Cooking instructions:
Soak wakame in water for a few minutes, remove and bring the water to the boil. Add finely chopped onions and wakame, radishes and carrots, cut into thin strips, and simmer for another 10 minutes. Dissolve miso in a little cooled cooking water and add it at the end. Sprinkle with parsley and spring onions.

9.22 Kidney bean pot with lamb and sage

Nourishes Yin from heart and kidney, strengthens spleen and kidney Yang, forces Qi, heats middle and lower heater, dissolves stagnation, directs upwards, moisturizes, relaxes, builds up Qi, spreads.
Cooking time approx. 1 1/2 hours
Calories p. portion: 391
4 portions
Allergens: F

Quantity of ingredients
Soybean oil 2 table spoons / 30g. (yes).....................................earth
Onion white 2 pieces / 120g. (yes)..metal
Lamb meat 5/8 oz / 200g. (yes)...fire
Sage 4-5 leaves / 2g. (little)..fire
Salt 1 pinch / 0,5g. (recommended)...water
Rosemary 1/2 teaspoon / 2g. (recommended)............................fire
Thyme 1/2 teaspoon / 2g. (recommended) ....*
Kidney beans (red) 5/8 lbs - 8oz / 250g. (recommended)...........water
Water 3 cups / 750g. (yes) ....earth

Cooking instructions:
Soak kidney beans in water overnight and strain.
In a saucepan with oil, roast the onion. Dice the lamb and place in the pot.
Season with salt, sage, rosemary and thyme.
Roast lamb well and cover pot. Cook over low heat and add ten-quarters of a gallon (750ml.) of cold water after 10 minutes.
Salt again.
Heat till it boils. Add beans to it.
Simmer for at least 1 hour until the beans and meat are tender.

9.23 Leek soup with almondmash

Gets Qi moving, moisten the lungs and large intestine, cools heat, preserves the fluids, contracts, forces Qi, forces spleen, relieves inflammation, moisturizes, relaxes, spreads.
Cooking time approx. 20 min
Calories p. portion: 115
4 portions
Allergens: HN

Quantity of ingredients

Water 2 cup / 480g. (yes).. earth
Sugar cane sugar 1 pinch / 0,3g. (little) .... earth
Leek 2 pieces / 400g. (recommended)...................................... metal
Salt 1 pinch / 0,5g. (recommended)... water
Lemon juice 1/2 piece / 15g. .... wood
Rosemary 1 Twig / 3g. (recommended)... fire
Pepper powder (hot) Alternative to rosemary / g. (recommended). fire
Potato flour 1 table spoon / 8g. (recommended) .... earth
Almond puree 2 table spoons / 20g. (yes)................................... earth
Sesame oil few drops / 1g. (recommended).............................. earth
Pepper white (ground) 1 pinch / 0,2g. (yes) .... metal

Cooking instructions:

Add a pinch of sugar to hot water, add chopped leeks and a pinch of salt; simmer until the leek is half cooked; season with lemon juice, fresh rosemary or rose paprika.

Dissolve potato flour separately in cold water; thicken the soup with it.

Add almond purée, a few drops of toasted sesame oil, pepper and simmer until the leek is cooked.

Add mushrooms; they build up juices and soften the yangling effect of the leeks.

9.24 Lentils and rice stew

Strengthens spleen and liver, regulates Qi flow, moisturizes, relaxes, builds up Qi, spreads, warms the stomach and spleen, harmonizes the intestine, forces Qi, reduces moisture, brings the liver Qi in motion, cools heat.
Cooking time approx. 25 min
Calories p. portion: 232
3 portions
Allergens: LNO

Quantity of ingredients

Lentils 1/4 lbs - 4oz / 100g. (recommended) .... water
Water 5 cups / 500g. (yes) .... earth
Rice variety any 1 cup / 120g. (yes)... metal
Sesame oil 1 table spoon / 10g. (recommended)....................... earth
Carrot 2 pieces / 150g. (recommended).................................... earth

Celery sticks 2 rods / 20g. (little)... earth
Cumin (Caraway seed) 1 pinch / 0,2g. (yes) .... metal
Salt 1 pinch / 0,5g. (recommended).. water
Vinegar (Apple vinegar) 1 dash / 2g. (little) .... wood
Parsley 2 table spoons / 18g. (recommended)........................... wood

Cooking instructions:
Soak the dry lentils the day before.
Heat sesame oil in a hot pot; cut carrot and celery into small pieces and
sauté; add rice, a pinch of cumin and lentils and heat till it boils.
If the lenses are soft, add salt; season with a little vinegar and garnish
with parsley.

Variant: In summer you can omit the cumin and add fresh green peas,
Chinese cabbage or celery.

9.25 Lights with chopped root vegetables
Nourishes and forces lungs, forces Qi.
Cooking time approx. 1 1/2 hours
Calories p. portion: 199
8 portions
Allergens: ADGLMO

Quantity of ingredients
Beef lungs (calf) 2 lbs / 900g. (yes) .... earth
Celery root 1/8 lbs - 2oz / 50g. (recommended) .... earth
Leek 1/2 oz / 20g. (recommended)... metal
Parsnip 1/8 lbs - 2oz / 50g. (recommended) .... fire
Carrot 1/8 lbs - 2oz / 50g. (recommended) .... earth
Parsley root 1/8 lbs - 2oz / 50g. (recommended)........................ earth
Onion white 1 piece / 50g. (yes) .... metal
Bay leaf 1 Leaf / 1g. (recommended).. *
Peppercorns 5 pieces / 2g. (yes).. metal
Thyme 2 twigs / 5g. (recommended).. *
Garlic 1 clove / 2g. (little)... metal
Salt 1 teaspoon / 2g. (recommended)... water
Pepper (ground) 1 pinch / 0,5g. (yes) .... metal
Water 8 cup - 1/2 1 Gallons / 1900g. (yes)................................. earth
Lemon 1/4 / 10g. .... wood
Onion white 1 piece / 50g. (yes) .... metal
Pickle 2 pieces / 10g. (recommended).. wood
Capers in olive oil 6 pieces / 5g. (recommended)......................... fire

Anchovy / Sardine 1 file (inserted in oil) / 8g. (little)....................water
Parsley 1 teaspoon / 3g. (recommended) ....wood
Marjoram 1 pinch / 1g. (yes)..metal
Lemon peel 1 piece grated / 1g. (little).. fire
Butter organic 1/8 lbs - 2oz / 60g. (recommended)..................... earth
Wheat flour 1/8 lbs - 2oz / 40g. (little) ....wood
Vinegar (Apple vinegar) 1 table spoon / 10g. (little)...................wood
Mustard 1 teaspoon / 3g. (recommended) ....metal
Sugar white 1 teaspoon / 3g. .... earth
Peppers (sweet) 1 teaspoon / 2g. (recommended)..................... earth
Marjoram 1 teaspoon / 2g. (yes)...metal

Cooking instructions:

Wash lungs. Clean vegetables, wash, cut into pieces. Cook lungs in 2
liters of water with salt, bay leaf, some peppercorns, thyme, whole,
peeled onion, clove of garlic and vegetables, turn after 20 min. If there
is no light drop at a fork penetration, remove the lungs and place in cold
water. Strain the brew and let it boil down. Cut the Lungs in not too thin
slices, these cut into fine noodles. Mix with salt, pepper, juice of quarter
lemon and set aside.
Sauce: Chop the small onion, gherkins, six capers, anchovy fillets,
parsley, a quarter lemon and a little marjoram very finely. In melted
butter roast the flour dark brown, add the finely chopped and roast
briefly. Quench with vinegar, pour in the broth, stir well with the whisk,
simmer gently for about 20 minutes.
Add the sliced lungs, season to taste with mustard, sugar until spicy,
add rose paprika and marjoram to taste and infuse for another quarter
of an hour. Serve with napkin or bread dumplings.

9.26 Millet mash with steamed pears

Moisturizes lungs, cools heat, reduces lung mucus, produces humors,
moisturizes, relaxes, builds up Qi, spreads, strengthens spleen and
kidney, diuretic.
Cooking time approx. 25 min
Calories p. portion: 235
3 portions

Quantity of ingredients

Millet 1 cup / 100g. (little)... earth
Water 1 1/2 cups / 220g. (yes)... earth
Cardamom 1 pinch / 0,5g. (recommended)......................................*
Pear 1-2 pcs. Biological / 250g. (recommended)....................... earth

Salt 1 pinch / 0,2g. (recommended)...water
Grape juice red 1 cup / 250g. (recommended)........................... earth
Cinnamon ground 1 pinch / 0,2g. (recommended) ....*
Clove 2 pieces / 0,4g. (yes)...metal
Lemon juice 1 table spoon / 8g. .... wood

Cooking instructions:
Roast millet while stirring until it smells well.
Cool the pot briefly.
Add 2 cups of hot water, the cardamom and a pinch of salt.
On low flame, covered, for 20 min. simmer.
Quarter the pears, remove the core, peel on request, add about ¼ liter
of red grape juice, cinnamon stick, cloves, lemon juice and a pinch of
salt) and simmer gently covered for a few minutes.

9.27 Millet with egg and butter

Forces blood, Yin and Jing, nourishes Yin, moisturizes in case of
internal dryness, forces blood, forces spleen, calms nerves and
stomach, strengthens spleen and kidney, diuretic, strengthens Qi and
kidney Jing, moisturizes, relaxes, builds up Qi, spreads.
Cooking time approx. 25 min
Calories p. portion: 338
2 portions
Allergens: CG

Quantity of ingredients
Millet 1 cup / 100g. (little).. earth
Ginger fresh 1/2 teaspoon / 1g. (recommended)........................metal
Salt 1 pinch / 0,5g. (recommended)...water
Parsley 2 table spoons / 16g. (recommended)........................... wood
Pepper powder (hot) 1 pinch / 1g. (recommended) .... fire
Chicken egg 2 pieces / 100g. (recommended)........................... earth
Butter organic 2 table spoons / 20g. (recommended)................. earth
Nutmeg 1 pinch / 0,2g. (little)...metal
Water 1 1/2 cups / 200g. (yes)... earth

Cooking instructions:
Simmer the millet with the ginger and nutmeg in the water for 5 min.
and let it swell for another 30 min.
Cook and peel 1 soft egg per person; pile up the millet on plates and
place 1 egg each in a hollow in the millet mountain; Put butterflakes
over it. Sprinkle with chopped parsley and the rose paprika.

9.28 Pear compote

Moisturizes lungs, reduces lung mucus, nourishes lungs Qi.
Cooking time approx. 20 min
Calories p. portion: 100
3 portions

Quantity of ingredients
Water 1 1/2 cups / 240g. (yes)... earth
Pear 4 / 500g. (recommended).. earth

Cooking instructions:
Halve organic pears. Cores and skin can be used. Pear in the pot and add water. Simmer for up to 20 minutes until pears are tender.

9.29 Pear juice

Moisturizes lungs, reduces lung mucus, nourishes lungs Qi.
Cooking time approx. 5 min
Calories p. portion: 180
2 portions

Quantity of ingredients
Pear 3 pieces / 600g. (recommended)....................................... earth

Cooking instructions:
Peel pears thinly (vitamins under the skin) and core. Juice in the juicer.

9.30 Radish with spring onions and carrots

Nutritious, moisturizing and dynamizing, moves Qi and blood, dissolves stagnation, directs upwards, strengthens stomach Qi, diuretic, moisturizes, relaxes, builds up Qi, spreads. regulates Qi, warms spleen and kidney.
Cooking time approx. 30 min
Calories p. portion: 246
2 portions
Allergens: EG

Quantity of ingredients
Carrot 2 pieces / 200g. (recommended)..................................... earth
Radish black 1/2 piece / 100g. (recommended) .... metal
Ginger powder 1 knife tip / 0,2g. (little) .... metal
Onion (spring onion) 1 piece / 20g. (yes) .... metal

Salt 1 pinch / 0,5g. (recommended)...water
Soy sauce 1 dash / 2g. ....water
Lemon juice 2 table spoons / 16g. .... wood
Curcuma 1 pinch / 0,2g. (little)...*
Pepper powder (hot) 1 pinch / 0,2g. (recommended) .... fire
Butter organic 1 teaspoon / 3g. (recommended) .... earth
Water 1 cup / 250g. (yes).. earth
Corn Grease (Polenta) 1 cup / 100g. (little)............................... earth
Salt 1 pinch / 0,5g. (recommended)...water

Cooking instructions:

Cook finely chopped carrots, black or white finely chopped radish, a pinch of grated ginger. Steam for 10 minutes, then strain.
In the meantime stir in chopped spring onions, salt, soy sauce, a little lemon juice, a pinch of turmeric or rose paprika and a piece of butter.

Garnish:
Stir the polenta into a pot of hot water, stirring constantly, until the polenta has the desired texture. Pull the polenta off the fire and let it swell for about 10 minutes.

9.31 Reissue soup with fresh fruits

Forces kidney and bladder, strengthens Qi and kidney Jing, moisturizes, relaxes, builds up Qi, reduces internal heat, produces humors, moisturizes, spreads, expels cold, dissolves stagnation, drives sweat, stimulates nerves.
Cooking time approx. 1 1/2 hours
Calories p. portion: 143
4 portions
Allergens: G

Quantity of ingredients

Rice wild (nature rice) 1 cup / 100g. (yes)...................................metal
Water 8 cups / 900g. (yes) .... earth
Apple (sweet) 1 1/2 cups / 200g. (little)...................................... earth
Butter organic 1 table spoon / 10g. (recommended)................... earth
Vanilla 1 pinch / 0,2g. (recommended) ....*
Sugar cane sugar 2 teaspoons / 6g. (little)................................ earth

Cooking instructions:
Prepare rice congee according to basic recipe.

At the end, add finely chopped fruits to the season, vanilla, chili and butter; sweet to taste.

Variant: With nuts, the dish can always be made richer and more filling.

Effect: Cooked or steamed fruits are easier to digest and act better than raw. For some fruits, which are particularly suitable for hot summer days - such as melons and berries - it is still advisable to add the fruits only to a hot porridge.
Other types of fruit - such as apples, pears, plums and cherries - can also be simmered for a while.

9.32 Rice congee with carrots and fennel

Nutritious builds up Qi, forces the digestive functions.
Cooking time approx. 2 hours and more
Calories p. portion: 131
3 portions
Allergens: G

Quantity of ingredients
Basic recipe for a rice soup (Congee) 2 cup / 500g. (recommended) *
Carrot 2 pieces / 100g. (recommended).................................... earth
Fennel 1 piece / 250g. (recommended) .... earth
Butter organic 1 teaspoon / 3g. (recommended) .... earth
Cardamom 1/2 teaspoon / 1g. (recommended)................................ *

Cooking instructions:
Cook rice congee according to basic recipe.
Clean and cut carrots and fennel.

When carrots and fennel are cooked from the beginning, they serve wholesomeness. If added shortly before the end of the cooking time, taste and vitamins are retained.

Refine with butter and cardamom before serving.

9.33 Rice congee with crushed walnuts

Nourishing and slightly warming, warms the middle, builds up Qi, warms the stomach and spleen, harmonizes the intestine, forces Qi, reduces moisture.
Cooking time approx. 2 hours and more
Calories p. portion: 406
2 portions
Allergens: H

Quantity of ingredients
Basic recipe for a rice soup (Congee) 4 cups / 500g. (recommended)*
Sugar cane sugar 2 table spoons / 20g. (little) .... earth
Walnuts 1 cup / 70g. (yes) .... earth
Cinnamon ground 1 pinch / 0,2g. (recommended) .... *

Cooking instructions:
Cook the basic recipe for rice soup (congee)
Note: The crushed walnuts can be cooked from the beginning.
Variation: Refine with sweet or spicy ingredients as you like. In particular, cinnamon, cloves, and ginger increase the warming effect and wholesomeness.

9.34 Rice congee with dried fruit

Warms the stomach and spleen, harmonizes the intestine, forces Qi, reduces moisture, nourishes blood and Yi, harmonizes lungs Qi, strengthens Qi and kidney Jing, moisturizes, relaxes, builds up Qi, spreads.
Cooking time approx. 10 min
Calories p. portion: 210
2 portions
Allergens: GO

Quantity of ingredients
Basic recipe for a rice soup (Congee) 4 cups / 500g. (recommended)*
Butter organic 1/2 teaspoon / 5g. (recommended) .... earth
Apricot dried 6 table spoons / 50g. (recommended) .... earth
Water 1/2 cup / 50g. (yes) .... earth
Maple syrup 1 dash / 3g. (little) .... earth

Cooking instructions:
Cook rice congee according to basic recipe.
Melt a small amount of butter over a low heat and briefly fry small dried

fruit with 1/2 cup of water. Add the amount of rice porridge desired for the meal and heat. Serve hot and sweeten with maple syrup if necessary.
Variant: In addition fresh fruit with braise.

9.35 Rice congee with honey pear and black sesame

Especially good in kidney Yin deficiency, moisturizes lungs, cools heat, reduces lung mucus, produces humors, moisturizes, relaxes, builds up Qi, spreads, moisturizes intestines, nourishes Yin.
Cooking time approx. 10 min - 3 hours
Calories p. portion: 158
2 portions
Allergens: N

Quantity of ingredients
Basic recipe for a rice soup 1 1/2 cups / 240g. (recommended) .... *
Pear 2 pieces / 300g. (recommended) .... earth
Sesame, black 1 teaspoon / 3g. (recommended) .... wood

Cooking instructions:
Cook rice congee according to basic recipe.
Fill pot with 3 cm of water and heat till it boils. Quarter the pears (with the skin and seeds) and simmer them covered with black sesame for 10 minutes. Mix with the rice.

9.36 Rice dulse soup

Strengthens spleen and liver, regulates Qi flow, relaxes, builds up Qi, spreads, dries out, passes downwardly, strengthens stomach Qi, warms the stomach and spleen, harmonizes the intestine, forces Qi, reduces moisture.
Cooking time approx. 5 min
Calories p. portion: 190
2 portions
Allergens: L

Quantity of ingredients
Basic recipe for a rice soup 4 cups / 500g. (recommended) .... *
Basic recipe for a vegetable soup 2 cup / 500g. (recommended) ...... *
Dulse (seaweed) 2 table spoons / 15g. (recommended) .... water

Cooking instructions:
Worm up a portion of pre-cooked basic recipe for a ricesoupe (congee) and a portion pre-cooked basic recipe for a vegetable soup.
Bake the dulse in the oven at 220 degrees for 3 minutes. Spread the crisp dulse over the rice.

9.37 Rice noodle soup with shiitake mushrooms

Strengthens spleen and liver, regulates Qi flow, relaxes, builds up Qi, spreads, dries out, passes downwardly, strengthens stomach Qi, nourishes Yin of the lungs, stomach and colon, supports digestion, reduces internal wind.
Cooking time approx. 20 min
Calories p. portion: 66
2 portions
Allergens: L

Quantity of ingredients
Rice noodles 2 handful / 20g. (yes) ....metal
Shiitake, dried 4-6 pieces / 5g. (recommended)......................... earth
Basic recipe for a vegetable soup 1 1/2 cups / 240g. (recommended)*
Chinese cabbage 1 cup / 60g. (recommended).......................... earth
Lovage 1 teaspoon / 3g. (recommended) ....metal
Miso 2 table spoons / 18g. (recommended) ....water

Cooking instructions:
Soak rice noodles and shiitake mushrooms separately in cold water. Heat the vegetable broth and add the soaked shiitake mushrooms cut into strips and simmer gently. Cut Chinese cabbage into noodles, add lovage green and rice noodles and let it steep for a while. Before serving, stir in Miso dissolved in a little cooled water. Recommendation: Suitable at the beginning of each meal, also for breakfast

9.38 Rice soup with grated carrots and fresh herbs

Strengthens spleen and liver, regulates Qi flow, moisturizes, relaxes, builds up Qi, spreads, forces kidney and bladder.
Cooking time approx. 5 min
Calories p. portion: 131
4 portions
Allergens: EG

Quantity of ingredients

Rice wild (nature rice) 1 cup / 100g. (yes)................................metal
Water 6 cups / 700g. (yes) .... earth
Carrot 1 piece / 100g. (recommended) .... earth
Soy sauce 1 dash / 2g. ....water
Butter organic 1 teaspoon / 3g. (recommended) .... earth
Ground 1 pinch / 0,3g. (recommended) .... earth
Curcuma 1 pinch / 0,2g. (little)...*
Herbs various 1 teaspoon (chopped) / 3g. (recommended)...............*

Cooking instructions:

In a portion of rice congee according to basic recipe, softly cook a grated carrot, add butter and soy sauce.
Sprinkle with fresh herbs.
Spices and herbs: black cumin, turmeric, cardamom, parsley, sage, thyme, basil, rosemary.
Winter: parsnip, celery, onion, leek, pumpkin
Summer: tomatoes, zucchini, spring onion, radishes, arugula.

9.39 Rice with stewed vegetables

Dissipates heat and moisture.
Cooking time approx. 20 min
Calories p. portion: 166
2 portions
Allergens: L

Quantity of ingredients

Rice variety any 1/2 cup / 60g. (yes)..metal
Water 3 cups / 300g. (yes) .... earth
Lemon peel 1 piece / 3g. (little).. fire
Water 1/2 cup / 0g. (yes) .... earth
Carrot 2 pieces / 180g. (recommended)..................................... earth
Celery sticks 1/2 piece / 5g. (little) .... earth
Champignon 1/2 cup / 50g. (recommended) .... earth
Cress 2 table spoons / 20g. (recommended) ....metal
Linseed oil 1 dash / 3g. (recommended)..................................... earth

Cooking instructions:

Cook rice according to basic recipe with a piece of lemon peel.
Steam chopped carrots, celery and mushrooms until soft.
Then sprinkle with cress. Then add a dash of high quality cold oil.

9.40 Roasted oatmeal with grapes compote

Moisturizes, relaxes, builds up Qi, spreads, forces Qi, warms the stomach and spleen, promotes blood circulation and conduction flow.
Cooking time approx. 25 min
Calories p. portion: 328
2 portions
Allergens: AO

Quantity of ingredients
Oat flakes roasted 1 cup / 120g. (recommended) ....metal
Grapes red 1 1/2 cups / 240g. (recommended)........................... earth
Ginger fresh 1/2 teaspoon / 1g. (recommended)........................metal
Raisins 2 table spoons / 20g. (yes)...................................... earth
Cinnamon ground 1 pinch / 1g. (recommended) ....*
Water 1 1/2 cups / 200g. (yes).. earth

Cooking instructions:
Roast the oats briefly, pour over water, add raisins and cook while stirring for 20 min. Add grapes, ginger and cinnamon.

9.41 Sliced lamb with rosemary potatoes

Strengthens spleen and kidney Yang and stomach Qi, relieves weakness, heats middle and lower heater, forces Qi, relieves inflammation, moisturizes, relaxes, builds up Qi, spreads.
Cooking time approx. 1 hour
Calories p. portion: 461
4 portions
Allergens: LO

Quantity of ingredients
Lamb meat 7/8 lbs - 1 lbs / 500g. (yes).. fire
Olive oil 2 table spoons / 20g. (little).. earth
Onion white 1 piece / 50g. (yes) ....metal
Garlic 1 clove / 2g. (little)..metal
Nutmeg 1 pinch / 0,2g. (little)..metal
Carrot 3 pieces / 150g. (recommended)..................................... earth
Celery root 1/4 tuber / 120g. (recommended) .... earth
Rosemary 1 Twig / 3g. (recommended).. fire
Savory 1 teaspoon / 2g. (recommended)...................................water
Parsley 1 table spoon / 8g. (recommended)..............................wood
Pepper powder (hot) 1 pinch / 2g. (recommended) .... fire
Red wine 1/2 cup / 125g. (little) .... fire

Salt (herbal) 1 pinch / 1g. (recommended).................................water
Lemon juice 1/2 piece / 15g. ....wood
Cranberry 1 table spoon / 10g. (little)...wood
Potato 6 pieces / 400g. (recommended) .... earth

Cooking instructions:
Cut the lamb into strips, cut the carrots and celery into small cubes.
Heat the olive oil in a pan, fry the lamb in it, add the cut onions and
garlic, salt with herbal salt, a little water, parsley, deglaze with red wine,
season with paprika and small cut rosemary, mugwort, savory, carrots
and celery, turn the heat back on small Simmer for about 35 minutes.
Season with pepper and nutmeg, if necessary still salt, add a little
lemon juice, season with paprika, cranberries.

Cut the potatoes in half, the length of, spread a little olive oil on the cut
surface, salt, sprinkle 2-3 rosemary needles on each half potato, place
the potatoes on the baking sheet and bake in a preheated oven for
approx. 25 minutes at 190°C/374°F.

9.42 Tea from cinnamon sticks

Warms the stomach and spleen, promotes blood circulation and
conduction flow, relieves cold-sickness and pain.
Cooking time approx. 15 min
Calories p. portion: 2
1 portions

Quantity of ingredients
Cinnamon sticks 1/4 piece / 1g. (recommended) ....*
Water 1 cup / 125g. (yes) .... earth

Cooking instructions:
A quarter of a cinnamon stick for a cup of tea. Start cold and bring to
the boil. Let it sit for 15 minutes, then strain.
This tea is unsweetened and swallowed, slowly drunk. The amount is
enough for one day.

9.43 Tea from ginseng

Forces heart, lungs, stomach, spleen, kidney-Qi.
Cooking time approx. 20 min
Calories p. portion: 0
4 portions

Quantity of ingredients
Ginseng 2 teabags / 4g. (recommended)...*
Water 2 cup / 500g. (yes) .... earth

Cooking instructions:
A very mild form of taking ginseng is achieved by placing it in a thermos
of hot water. You can also use the root several times, not just for a pot
filling. Ideally, you should have cooked the water for 10 minutes - it is
then assigned to the conversion phase of fire (TCM) - and to use non-
carbonated medicinal spring water, if the quality of the water on site is
not good.
Ingestion: This mild ginseng tea can be drunk throughout the day for
strengthening.

9.44 Tea from licorice (heart-strengthening)

Strengthen spleen and stomach Qi, nourishes Yin from heart and
kidney, moisturizes, forces heart and kidney, reduces internal heat,
preserves the fluids, contracts.
Cooking time approx. 15 min
Calories p. portion: 20
4 portions

Quantity of ingredients
Licorice root tea 2-4 teaspoons / 6g. (recommended) ....*
Dates red 2 table spoons (chopped) / 20g. (recommended)....... earth
Wheat 2 teaspoons (milled) / 16g. (little)....................................wood
Water 2 cup / 500g. (yes) .... earth

Cooking instructions:
Simmer licorice root, red dates and wheat for 40 minutes, strain and
keep the tea in the refrigerator. Throw away the ingredients.
Variant: This recipe can be supplemented with chicken broth; it will be
even stronger.
Decoction: 2-4 teaspoons, sprinkle licorice with 1/2 liter of cold water,
heat till it boils, cook for 1 min, leave for 10 min. Drink 1 cup twice a
day.

9.45 Tea from longane

Forces spleen, builds up lung, builds up heart, calms nerves.
Cooking time approx. 10 min
Calories p. portion: 0
4 portions

Quantity of ingredients
Longane 2 teaspoons / 4g. (little).. *
Water 2 cup / 500g. (yes) .... earth

Cooking instructions:
Heat the water till it boils and put it aside. Add Longane and 10 min. to let go. Sweet to taste with honey. Strain when pouring.

9.46 Tea from thyme

Converts mucus, forces lungs and spleen, dries out, passes downwardly.
Cooking time approx. 10 min
Calories p. portion: 0
4 portions

Quantity of ingredients
Thyme 3 table spoons / 6g. (recommended)...................................... *
Water 2 cup water / 500g. (yes).. earth

Cooking instructions:
Heat the water till it boils and put it aside. Add thyme and 10 min. to let go. Strain. Sweet to taste with honey.
Drink 2 to 3 cups daily by mouth

9.47 Thick pea soup

Nourishes Qi, diuretic, harmonizes Qi (especially in the Middle and Lower), strengthens the kidney and the defense Qi, discards moisture.
Cooking time approx. 2-3 hours
Calories p. portion: 123
3 portions
Allergens: AN

Quantity of ingredients
Peas, green 3/8 lbs - 6oz / 150g. (recommended) ....water
Water 2 1/4 cups / 550g. (yes).. earth

Sesame oil 1 table spoon / 20g. (recommended)....................... earth
Onion white 1/2 piece / 25g. (yes) ....metal
Ginger fresh 1/2 teaspoon / 1g. (recommended)........................metal
Ground 1/2 teaspoon / 1g. (recommended) .... earth
Oat meal 1 table spoon / 15g. (yes)..metal
Salt 1 pinch / 1g. (recommended)..water
Parsley 1 stem / 2g. (recommended).. wood

Cooking instructions:
Soak dried peas before cooking. Sauté sesame oil, onion, a little
oatmeal, ginger and cumin in a hot pot; add the peas and simmer for 2-
3 hours; add salt at the end and pruée with a blender; garnish with
parsley.

9.48 Turkey breast with vegetables (Asian)

Forces Qi, blood and Jing, middle heater, forces essence, contracts,
warms the stomach and spleen, harmonizes the intestine, forces Qi,
reduces moisture, regulates Qi, warms spleen and kidney, dissolves
stagnation, directs upwards.
Cooking time approx. 45 min
Calories p. portion: 535
2 portions
Allergens: AEN

Quantity of ingredients
Rice variety any 1 cup / 120g. (yes)...metal
Water 6 cups / 240g. (yes) .... earth
Turkey breast meat 5/8 oz / 200g. (recommended).................... earth
Ginger fresh 1/3 inch / 3g. (recommended)................................metal
Garlic 1 piece / 2g. (little)...metal
Soy sauce 2 table spoons / 20g. ....water
Wheat flour 2 teaspoons / 15g. (little) .... wood
Onion (spring onion) 2 pieces / 40g. (yes) ....metal
Peppers 1/2 piece / 10g. (yes)... earth
Champignon 8 pieces / 30g. (recommended) .... earth
Sesame oil 2 table spoons / 20g. (recommended) .... earth
Soy sauce 1 table spoon / 12g. ....water
Curry 1 pinch / 2g. ....metal
Turmeric (yellow root) 1 pinch / 2g. (recommended) ....*
Cashews 2 teaspoons / 25g. (little).. earth

Cooking instructions:
Cook the rice in salted water.
Cut the turkey meat into thin strips. Peel and dice the ginger and garlic.
Put together with the meat strips in a bowl. Mix 1 tbsp of soy sauce with
the wheat starch and stir until smooth. Add to the meat and marinate for
30 minutes. Wash spring onions and peppers, clean and cut into small
pieces. Clean and quarter the mushrooms.
Put one tablespoon of sesame oil in a pan and sauté and warm the
marinated turkey. Now add the remaining oil to the pan and fry the other
vegetables in it. Now add the meat and season with soy sauce and
spices. Serve with the rice. Sprinkle the cashews over the dish before
serving.

9.49 Warming porridge

Forces Qi and defensive power.
Cooking time approx. 10 min
Calories p. portion: 357
1 portions
Allergens: AHO

Quantity of ingredients
Oat flakes (whole grain) 6 table spoons / 60g. (recommended)..metal
Fig dried 3 pieces / 15g. (recommended).................................. earth
Star anise 1 piece / 1g. (yes)... *
Ginger fresh 1 pinch / 0,5g. (recommended)............................metal
Water 1 cup / 120g. (yes)... earth
Maple syrup 1 table spoon / 10g. (little) .... earth
Walnuts 1 table spoon (chopped) / 8g. (yes)............................. earth

Cooking instructions:
Soak the dried fruit. Roast Oatmeal dry. Add dried ginger, star anise or
cinnamon, a little grated ginger and boil everything with water to a
mash. With maple syrup sweet. Whip grated walnuts and sprinkle
before serving.

Effect: Suitable for the cold season.
Caution: Fresh ginger does not drink over a long period of time.

10 Effects of food

10.1 Use ingredients: recommendable

Acai powder
Acerola fruit nectar or powder
Agave nectar
Agrimony
Almond
Aloe juice
Amaranth Pops
Angelica root
Apple puree
Apricot dried
Apricot jam
Apricot nectar
Apricots juice
Baking powder
Banchatee (green tea)
barberry
Barley flour
Barley grass powder
Barley grouts
Barley malt
Barley not peeled
Basic recipe for a beef soup
Basic recipe for a beef soup (warming)
Basic recipe for a chicken soup (warming)
Basic recipe for a duck soup
Basic recipe for a fish soup
Basic recipe for a rice soup (Congee)
Basic recipe for a vegetable soup (nutritious)
Basil
Basil (fresh)
Batavia
Bay leaf
Bean oil
Beans (green, fresh)
Bearberry leaf
Beef bone marrow
Beef heart
Beef heart (calf)
Beef kidney
Beef liver
Beef meat (calf)
Beef Oxtail pieces
Beef soup meat
Beer (alcohol-free)
Beer (alcohol-reduced)
Berries of the season
Berry juice

Bitter Herb liqueur
Bitter Lemon
Bitter liqueur
Bitter orange peel
Black beans
Black caraway
Black fungus mushroom
Blackberry dried (unripe fruit)
Blackberry jam
Blackberry leaves
Black-eyed peas
Blackthorn (Sloe)
Blue mallow tee
Blueberry dried
Blueberry jam
Bocksdorn fruits (Fructus Lycii, Goji, goji berry dried
Boletus mushroom
Borage
Borage oil
Brazil nuts
Bread roll
Bread with carob kernel flour
Breadcrumbs (wheat bread, bread roll)
Brie cheese
Broad beans (thick beans)
Broccoli
Brown ale
Brussels sprouts
Buckbean
Buckwheat (roasted) Kasha
Buckwheat whole grain
Bush beans
Butter (half fat)
Butter beans white
Butter organic
Camembert
Campari
Capers in olive oil
Cardamom
Carob flour, St. john's bread
Carp
Carrot
Carrot (Early Carrot)
Carrot juice without sugar
Cauliflower
Celery root
Chamomile tea
Champignon

Channa-Dal
Chanterelle
Chenpi (chinese tangerine bowl)
Cherry (sour)
Cherry compote
Chervil
Chervil dried
Chestnut puree
Chestnuts
Chicken Blood
Chicken egg
Chicken egg white
Chicken heart
Chicken liver
Chicken meat
Chicken stomach
Chicken yolk
Chickpeas
Chickweed
Chinese cabbage
Chinese pearl barley
Chives
Chocolate
Chocolate (Diabetic)
Chrysanthemum blossom tea
Cinnamon ground
Cinnamon sticks
Clarified butter
Clementine
Coconut fat
Coconut meat
Codfish
Cola drink
Cola drink (low calorie)
Compote (fruits of the season)
Cooking oil
Coriander
Coriander (fresh)
Corn (fast polenta)
Corn (roasted)
Corn flour
Corn germ oil
Corn silk tea
Corn starch
Cottage cheese
Cranberries
Cranberry
Cranberry jam
Cream (30% fat)
Cream 10% coffee cream
Cream sour 10%
Cream sour 20%
Cream sour 30%
Creamer

Créme fraiche cheese
Cress
Crispbread
Crucian
Cucumber (bitter)
Cucumber (spicy cucumber)
Currant jam (black)
Currant jam (red)
Currant juice (black)
Currants (black)
Currants (red)
Curry paste red
Daisy
Dandelion juice
Dashi
Dates red
Deer meat
Deer meat
Deer's Bones
Deer's kidneys
Dill
Ducks egg
Dulse (seaweed)
Dyer's broom herb
Edam cheese
Eel smoked
Elderberries
Emmental cheese
Evening primrose oil
Fennel
Fennel seeds ground
Fenugreek (Trigonella foenum-graecum)
Fernet Branca (herbal bitter liqueur)
Feta cheese
Fig
Fig dried
Fish innards
Fish pieces mixed (fresh water)
Fish remains
Fish sauce
Flounder
Flower pollen
Fox nut, gorgon nut, makhana
French beans
Fresh cheese from soya
Fresh cheese with herbs
Freshwater crab
Freshwater fish
Fructose (glucose)
Fruit mix juice
Fruit tea
Gail plum
Galangal

Garam Masala powder
Gelatin white
Gelee Royal
Gentian root
Gentian root tea
Ginger fresh
Ginger oil
Ginkgo fruit
Ginseng
Ginseng liqueur
Ginseng root
Goat and sheep's blood
Goat and sheep's brain
Goat and sheep's liver
Goat and sheep's stomach
Goose
Goose blood
Goose fat
Goose parts
Gorgonzola
Gouda cheese
Gourd
Grape juice red
Grape juice white
Grapefruit dried peel
Grapes red
Grapes white
Grapeseed oil
Greengage
Ground
Ground caraway
Guava
Halibut (Flatfish)
Hazelnuts
Herbal tea mix
Herbs bitter
Herbs of Provence
Herbs various
Herbs wild
Herring
Hibiscus
Hibiscus tea
Hijiki
Hokkaido pumpkin
Honey wine (Met)
Hop
Horehound leaves
Horse meat
Hyssop
Jasmine blossoms tee
Jellyfish
Kaki plum
Kalmus
Kidney beans (red)

King Solomon's-seal
Kohlrabi
Kudzu
Kukicha tea
Ladyfingers
Lamb kidneys
Lamb liver
Lamb's lettuce
Lavender blossoms
Leaf salads (bitter)
Leek
Lemon Balm (dried)
Lemon Balm (fresh)
Lemongrass
Lentils
Lentils black
Lentils yellow
Licorice root tea
Lily bulbs
Lima beans
Lime blossom tea
Linseed
Linseed (crushed)
Linseed oil
Liver smoothing tea
Loquate / Japanese medlar
Lotus roots
Lotus seeds
Lovage
Lovage seeds
Luo Han Guo fruit
Lychee liqueur
Lye roll
Mackerel
Malt
Mango juice
Manioc flour
Mare's milk
Margarine
Margarine (diet)
Martini
Mascarpone cheese
Mayonnaise 50%
Mayonnaise 80%
Mediterranean fish (cod, plaice, haddock, sea eel, mackerel)
Medlar
Mineral water
Mirabelle plum
Miso
Miso black (fermented)
Mixed Pickles
Morel (black, dried)
Morel, dried

Mu Erh Mushroom
Muesli
Mulled Wine Spice
Multi-grain bread (gray bread)
Mustard
Mustard Dijon
Mustard medium hot
Mustard sweet
Nasturtium (nose-twister or nose-tweaker)
Nectarine
Nettles
Noodles (wheat) with egg
Noodles (wheat, lasagne) with egg
Noodles (wheat, ribbon noodles) with egg
Noodles (wheat, spaghetti) with egg
Noodles (whole grain) with egg
Nori, purple seaweed, red algae
Oat flakes (whole grain)
Oat flakes roasted
Oat fusion (baby food)
Octopus
Olives green
Orange blossom
Orange dried peel
Orange grated peel
Orange jam
Orange peel
Oregano fresh
Oyster shell powder
Palm oil
Parsley
Parsley root
Parsnip
Passion blossoms tea
Passion fruit
Peanut (roasted)
Peanut butter
Peanut oil
Peanuts
Pear
Pear juice
Pearl barley
Peas
Peas, green
Pepper powder (hot)
Peppermint
Peppermint tea
Pepperoni
Pepperoni, red, pitted, halved
Pepperoni, yellow, pitted, halved
Peppers (sweet)
Peppers powder

Perch
Pickle
Pig blood
Pigeon egg
Pine nuts
Pinto beans speckled
Pistachios
Plum dried
Plums
Pork Bacon
Pork brain
Pork fat (lard)
Pork ham
Pork ham cooked
Pork ham smoked
Pork kidneys
Pork Lard
Pork liver
Pork lung
Pork marrow bones
Pork sausage (Bratwurst) Pork skin
Pork/beef sausage (smoked)
Pork's intestine
Potato
Potato (mealy)
Potato flour
Prickly pear
Processed cheese 12%
processed cheese 30%
Prosecco
Psyllium seed
Pudding powder vanilla
Puff pastry
Pumpernickel (dark bread)
Pumpkin
Pumpkin seeds
Quail
Quail egg
Rabbit (wild)
Rabbit meat
Radish black
Radish horseradish
Radish leaves
Rapeseed oil
Raspberry jam
Raspberry leaf tea
Red beet
Red berry (without sugar)
Red cabbage
Reishi mushroom
Ribworttea
Rice (fragrance)
Rice (Gaoliang / Sorghum)
Rice Basmati

Rice mash
Rice round grain
Rice starch
Rice sticky
Rose blossom tea
Rose hip
Rose leaf tea
Rosefish
Rosemary
Rum
Rusk
Rye wholemeal bread
Safflower (Dyer's thistle / Hong Hua)
Sake
Salt
Salt (herbal)
Savory
Savoy cabbage / kale
Sea buckthorn
Sea cucumber
Sesame oil
Sesame oil roasted
Sesame paste (Tahini)
Sesame, black
Sesame, white
Sheep's milk
Sheep's milk yoghurt
Sherry (whine)
Shiitake, dried
Shrimps
Skim milk powder
Slug
Sourdough
Soy flour
Soy noodles
Soy Tofu smoked
Soya Cuisine (soy cream)
Soybeans
Soybeans, blacks, fermented
Spelled flakes
Spirit
Spurdog (spiny dogfish, Schillerlocken)
St. Benedict's thistle, blessed thistle,
holy thistle, spotted thistle
Stevia (candyleaf, sweetleaf)
Strawberry jam
Sugar - icing sugar
Sugar molasses
Sugar palm sugar
Sugar substitute (sweetener)
Sunflower oil
Sunflower seeds
Supplementary nutrition
Sweet potato

Tabasco
Tea mixture uric acid lowering
Thistle oil
Thyme
Thyme dried
Toast bread (whole grain)
Tomato dried
Tomato juice
Tomato paste
Tomato puree
Tonic Water
Topinambur
Trout
Trout (smoked)
Truffle
Tsampa (roasted barley flour)
Turkey breast meat
Turkey ham
Turmeric (yellow root)
Turnip
Turnips
Umeboshi paste
Valerian
Vanilla
Vanilla pod
Vanilla powder
Vanilla sugar natural
Vinegar (Red wine vinegar)
Vinegar Aceto Balsamico
Vinegar Aceto Balsamico white
Walnut oil
Walnuts roasted
Water hot
Wax gourd
Wheat flatbread/pita bread
Wheat flour whole grain
Wheat germ oil
Wheat/Rye/Gray-black bread with yeast
Wheatgrass juice
Wheatgrass powder
Whey
White beans
White bread (baguette)
White bread (pretzel sticks)
White bread (roll)
White bread (wheat bread)
White breadcrumbs
White cabbage
White dumpling bread (wheat bread cut
into chunks)
Whitefish
Whole grain bread
Wholemeal flour
Wild boar meat

Wild garlic (garlic spinach)
Wild herbs
Wild strawberries
Wormwood
Wormwood herb

Yam root, yam root tuber
Yarrow
Yeast
Yew nut
Yoghurt vanilla

10.2 Use ingredients: yes

Adzuki beans
Almond marzipan
Almond milk
Almond puree
Anise (Common Fennel)
Apricot
Apricots
Beef fillet
Beef lungs (calf)
Beef meat
Beef meatbones
Beef stomach
Bulgur (cereals)
Cherry
Cherry juice
Clove
Couscous
Cumin (Caraway seed)
Dates dried
Eel
Fennel tea
Grass carp
Lamb bones
Lamb meat
Lamb shoulder
Lentils red
Marjoram
Mustard seeds
Oat
Oat flour
Oat meal
Oat milk
Okra
Olives
Onion (shallot)
Onion (spring onion)
Onion read
Onion white
Oyster mushroom

Peaches
Peaches (canned)
Pearl barley
Pepper (ground)
Pepper Cayenne
Pepper white (ground)
Peppercorns
Peppers
Pheasant
Pumpkin seed oil
Radish
Radish (white, green, purple-red)
Raisins
Rice (whole grain)
Rice black
Rice flour
Rice long grain rice
Rice malt
Rice noodles
Rice red
Rice sweet
Rice variety any
Rice wild (nature rice)
Rye
Rye flour
Sago (cereals)
Salmon
Shrimp
Sour milk cheese 20%
Soybean oil
Spelled (Dark) bread
Spelled semolina
Spelled wholemeal flour
Star anise
Tuna
Umeboshi plums (Japanese apricots)
Walnuts
Water
Zucchini

10.3 Use ingredients: little

Anchovy / Sardine
Apple (sour)
Apple (sweet)

Apple juice (natural cloudy)
Arrowroot
Artichoke

Balm
Beer (Pils)
Beer (Top-fermented German dark beer)
Blackberry´s
Blueberry
Blueberry juice
Boxhorn clover seeds
Buckwheat
Buttermilk
Calamari
Cashews
Celery sticks
Cereal coffee
Chamomile
Chicory
Chili (pod or ground)
Chlorella (fresh water)
Clementines
Cocoa
Coconut flakes
Coconut grated
Coconut milk
Coix (seeds) YiYi Ren
Corn
Corn Grease (Polenta)
Cranberry
Cranberry juice
Cream, sweet 30%
Curcuma
Curd cheese 20%
Curd cheese 40%
Currant (black)
Currant (red)
Currant (white)
Duck (heart)
Duck (slaughtered)
Feta cheese
Fresh cheese
Garlic
Ginger powder
Goat
Goat and sheep's milk
Goat cheese
Gooseberry
Green tea
Juniper berry
Kefir
Kombu seaweed (Saccharina japonica)
Lemon peel
Lobster
Longane
Mallow (Malva sylvestris) blossom tea

Maple syrup
Millet
Millet flakes
Mung bean
Mutton
Mutton
Nutmeg
Olive oil
Oregano dried
Oysters
Pomegranate
Poppy
Quince
Quinoa
Rabbit
Radicchio
Raspberry
Raspberry dried (immature)
Red wine
Romaine lettuce / lettuce salad
Saffron
Sage
Salsify
Sauerkraut (cutted cabbage fermented)
Sour cherries
Soy Tofu
Soybean milk
Soybeans, black
Soybeans, yellow
Spelled grain
Spiny lobsters
Strawberries
Strawberry Juice
Sugar brown
Sugar cane sugar
Sugar fructose - fruit sugar
Sugar glucose - grapes sugar
Sugar Milk Sugar
Tarragon (Estragon)
Vegetable juice
Vinegar (Apple vinegar)
Wakame
Wheat
Wheat bulgur
Wheat flakes
Wheat flour
Wheat semolina
Wheat semolina for children
White wine

10.4 Do not use contra-acting foods

Agar agar (kelp)
Amaranth
Asparagus (green or white)
Aubergine
Avocado
Bamboo shoots
Banana
Banana (cooking banana)
Barley
Black tea
Burdock root tea
Cantaloupe
Carambola (Star fruit)
Caviar
Chard
Cod
Coffee
Cow's milk (1.5% fat)
Cow's milk (whole milk 3.5% fat)
Crab
Cucumber
Curry
Dandelion (young plants)
Dandelionroots tea
Elderberry blossom tee
Endive salad
Goose egg
Grapefruit (Pomelo)
Grapefruit juice
Green spelt
Hawthorn
Honey
Iceberg lettuce
Kiwi
Kumquats
Lamb's lettuce
Lemon
Lemon juice
Lettuce
Lime
Lychee
Lychee in Preserved
Mango
Miso paste (soy bean paste)
Mold cheese

Mozzarella
Mulberry fruit
Mullet
Mung bean sprouting
Mussels
Octopus
Orange
Orange juice
Papaya
Parmesan
Peppers (rose peppers)
Pigeon
Pimento
Pineapple
Pineapple (from a can)
Pineapple juice without sugar
Plaice
Plum
Pork heart
Pork knuckle
Pork meat
Pork stomach
Rabbit liver
Rhubarb
Rose hip tea
Rucola
Seacrab
Shark
Sorrel
Sour cream 15% fat
Sour milk
Soy sauce
Spinach
Sugar candy white
Sugar white
Tangerine
Tomato
Watermelon
Wheat beer
Wheat bran
Yarrow tea
Yogi tea
Yogurt (natural, 1.5% fat)
Yogurt (natural, 3.5% fat)

11 Herbs and their effects

11.1 Basil

thermal effect: warm
taste: spicy, bitter
Dries out, leads down. Tonifies Yang and Qi, dissolves mucus-cold, eliminates wind-cold.
It has a beneficial effect on flatulence and nausea, relaxing and soothing. Good to fight emphysema, bronchitis, whooping cough, high blood pressure, headache, mouth odor, warts, hiccup, gout, migraine.

11.2 Mugwort

thermal effect: warm
taste: bitter, spicy
Regulates and nourishes bleeding, warms the inside, eliminates wind-cold, eliminates parasites, eliminates heat, wetness, regulates and moves Qi.
Reduces bleeding, alleviates pain. In the kitchen, mugwort is used as a spice for fat food. Since it contains many bitter substances, it boosts fat burning and promotes digestion.

11.3 Savory

thermal effect: warm
taste: bitter
Tonifies kidney yang, heart qi, stomach and spleen qi and warms the middle, moves the liver qi and blood, releases mucous and cold from the lungs, opens the surface, induces wind-cold.
Stomach-strengthening, soothing and appetizing. Ideal for prevent colds, strengthens the immun system. In case of incontinence or nocturnal wetting (not for children), put the beans in liquor for libido.

11.4 Coriander

thermal effect: warm
taste: spicy
Driving sweat, reducing wind, draining moisture, tonifying and regulating qi, eliminating wind-cold.
The essential oils are appetizing, digestive, cramping and soothing in stomach and intestinal disorders.

11.5 Herbs various

Stimulates appetite. Effect different.
Appetizing, lots of trace elements and vitamins.

11.6 Cress

thermal effect: cool
taste: sweet
Moves and tonifies qi and blood, diuretic, cools in internal heat,
moisturizes lungs, triggers stagnation, heads upwards.
Diuretic, supports urination. Good to fight dry mouth, inner agitation, sore
throat, diabetes, kidney stones, gastrointestinal complaints, lung
problems, menstrual cramps or cancer.

11.7 Chives

thermal effect: warm
taste: spicy
Directs upward. Tonifies blood, kidney Yang and Qi. Dissolves moisture.
Bactericide, prevents cancer, strengthens gastric juice production,
promotes digestion and blood circulation, promotes growth, triggers
stagnation.

11.8 Lovage

thermal effect: warm
taste: spicy, bitter
Reduces inner wind and moisture, dissolves stagnation, directs upward,
warms Yang, regulates and moves Qi, warms inside, dissolves mucus-
cold, eliminates wind-cold.
Stimulates digestion, reduces pain. Extracts of the root are used to flush
out urinary tract infections and prevent kidney gravel.

11.9 Lily bulbs

thermal effect: cool
taste: sweet, bitter
Tonifies Yin, soothes Shen / Spirit. Moisturizes the lungs, clears heat and
stops coughing.
Calms nerves, good to fight scaly skin. The onions and the petals are
added to ointments in the Orient, which can heal muscles and tendons.
White lily (astringent).

11.10   Marjoram

thermal effect: warm
taste: spicy
Dissolves stagnation, heads upwards. Regulates and moves Qi, eliminates wind-cold, dissolves slime-cold, calms down Shen / Spirit, suppresses inner wind, moves blood.
Helps to digest fat foods, strengthens digestive organs, helps to fight colds, strengthens menstruation, promotes skin healing.

11.11   Oregano fresh

thermal effect: warm
taste: bitter
Dries out, directs down, regulates and moves Qi, eliminates wind-cold, soothes Shen / Spirit, suppresses inner wind, warms inside, eliminates wind-cold / heat-wetness, moves blood, dissolves slime-cold.
It has an anti-digestive, calming and nerve-strengthening effect, helps to fight cramping stomach and intestinal disorders. The ingredient Carvacrol has an anti-inflammatory effect.

11.12   Parsley

thermal effect: warm
taste: bitter
Nourishes blood and liver, harmonizes liver and spleen, strengthens eyesight, preserves juices, contracts. Dissolves moisture and warms Yang.
Stimulates liver function, detoxifies. Forces urinating. Relieves flatulence. Digestive and menstrual stimulating, birth-
accelerating, memory-enhancing, blood-purifying, skin-smoothing.

11.13   Peppermint

thermal effect: cool
taste: spicy, bitter
Cools heat, expels mucus, dissipates wind-cold and wind-heat, moves stomach qi, releases congestion, tonifies, regulates and moves qi.
Relaxes, frees the lungs and the nose (inhale), regulates the cycle.
Stimulates bile flow and bile production, antispasmodic in gastrointestinal disorders, antimicrobial and antiviral.

11.14 Rosemary

thermal effect: warm
taste: bitter
Dries out, leads down. Strengthens the heart, lungs and spleen qi, strengthens liver blood. Strengthens heart-Yin. Expels spleen heat / cold moisture. Strengthens spleen and kidney yang.
Promotes digestion, relieves bloating, strengthens lung, spleen and kidney. Affects the circulation and nerves. Appetizing. Baths help to fight circulatory disorders as well as with gout and rheumatism.

11.15 Sage

thermal effect: neutral
taste: bitter, spicy
Expels slime, guides down, strengthens Qi, eliminates Wind-Heat, eliminate heat induced by Yin deficiency.
Good to fight yeast infections. The leaves have a digestive effect and are used in greasy foods. Antiperspirant effect. Helps to relieve coughing attacks. Dries out.

11.16 Black caraway

thermal effect: warm
taste: spicy, sweet
Dissolve / transform moisture, tonifyes Yang and Qi, moves blood, suppresses inner wind.
Detoxifying, immunoregulatory. In addition, the oil should stimulate the formation of bone marrow cells and generally protect body cells from viruses.

11.17 Thyme dried

thermal effect: warm
taste: bitter
Strengthens the lungs and spleen. Clears wind-cold, dissolves slime-cold, tones qi, soothes Shen / Spirit.
Disinfecting. It stimulates the blood circulation, increases the appetite and helps to digest fat meat better. Strengthens lungs and spleen.

11.18   King Solomon's-seal

thermal effect: neutral
taste: sweet, bitter
Tonifies Yin and Qi, astringent, tonifies blood, eliminates wind-cold / heat-wetness.
Used to repair wounds or damaged tissue. Good to fight dry cough, earlier also tuberculosis and dysentery, as well as diarrhea and hemorrhoids.

11.19   Yam root, yam root tuber

thermal effect: neutral
taste: sweet
Tonifies Yin, Yang and Qi, reduces inner wind, dissolves wetness, warms Yang.
Solves cramps (in the gastrointestinal tract). Digestive through increased bile production. Anti-inflammatory in rheumatic diseases.
Mucolytic agent for coughing. Relief of menopausal symptoms.

11.20   Lemongrass

thermal effect: taste:
Diverting, calming.
Reduction of flatulence, antimicrobial, appetizing. Prevention of influenza. Good to fight infections in the mouth and throat.

11.21   Lemon Balm (fresh)

thermal effect: cool
taste: sour
Soothes Shen / Spirit, regulates and moves Qi, eliminates heat caused by Yin deficiency, tones Qi.
Stimulating, antibacterial, encouraging, relaxing, antispasmodic, cooling, antipyretic, analgesic, sweat-inducing, virus-inhibiting. Good for colds, fever, flu, cough, bronchitis, asthma, loss of appetite, bloating, heartburn.

12 Basics of Nutrition

The basic principles of nutrition described herein are general recommendations. They are not aimed at a specific form of therapy. Recommendations concerning a therapy have priority.

12.1 Nutrition

Regular meals in a relaxed atmosphere. A warm breakfast is considered a good start into the day.
The main meals ought to be taken for lunch – supper in the early evening. Pay attention to feeling hungry or sated: don't eat too much nor remain hungry is the rule
Prepare the meals freshly from natural, regional products. Frozen, heat-conserved, industrially prepared or foodstuffs cooked in the microwave oven are rejected.
Choice of foodstuffs according to the season: more cooling food in summer, more warming food in winter.
Eat cooked food at least twice a day. Food and drinks ought to be lukewarm, never ice-cold or hot.
Raw vegetables, briefly cooked vegetables, freshly squeezed juices and mineral water are not recommended. Milk and dairy products are only included in the diet if they don't cause problems. Don't use therapeutic recipes over a longer period without consulting your doctor or therapist.

Varied food
Enjoy the diversity of foodstuffs. Characteristics of a balanced nutrition are variety, suitable combination and a balanced quantity of rich and low energy foodstuffs (on one hand avoiding undersupply with essential nutrients and on the other hand to take to many undesirable substances).

A lot of Cereal Products - and Potatoes
Bread, pasta, rice, cereal flakes (best wholemeal) as well as potatoes contain almost no fat, but many vitamins, mineral nutrients, trace elements, roughage and secondary plant substances. These foodstuffs ought to be taken with low-fat side dishes.

Vegetables and Fruit – „Take Five" every day ... 5 portions of vegetables and fruit a day, as fresh as possible, briefly cooked, or maybe one portion as a juice – ideal as a side dish to every meal as well as snack between meals: Thus a lot of vitamins, mineral nutrients as well as roughage and secondary plant substances

Daily milk and dairy products

Milk and Dairy Products every Day, once or twice per Week Fish; meat, sausages as well as eggs moderately. These foodstuffs contain valuable nutrients like calcium in the milk, iodine selenium and omega-3 fat acids in saltwater fish. Meat is favorable due to its high content of disposable iron and the vitamins B1, B6 and B12. Quantities of 300 – 600 g meat and sausage per week are sufficient. Prefer low-fat products, especially in meat- and dairy products.

Low-fat and fatty Foodstuffs

Fat supplies us with essential fat acids and fatty foodstuffs contain also fat-soluble vitamins. Fat is high in energy; therefore much fat in the food may cause overweight, possibly also cancer. Too many saturated fat acids may further a tendency for cardio-vascular diseases in the long term. Prefer vegetable oils and fats (e.g. rapeseed-, olive-, soya-oils and solid fats produced therefrom). Beware of invisible fat in meat- and dairy products, pastry and sweets as well as in fast-food and convenience foods. 70 – 90 g fat per day is sufficient.

Moderately Sugar and Salt

Take sugar and foods/drinks containing various kinds of sugar (e.g. glucose syrup) only occasionally. Use herbs and spices as well as a little salt creatively. Prefer salt containing iodine.

Plenty of Liquids

Water is absolutely essential. Drink 1-2 l liquids every day. Prefer water (with or without gas) and other low-calorie drinks. Alcoholic drinks should not be taken.

Tasty Dishes, carefully cooked

Cook the meals with as low temperatures and as short as possible, using little water and fat – this preserves the original taste, keeps the nutrients intact and prevents the production of harmful compounds.

Take time and enjoy the food

Take your Time and enjoy your Food
Eating consciously helps to eat right. The eye enjoys food, too. It's fun, invites to enjoy varied dishes and stimulates the feeling of satiety.

Watch your Weight and stay in Motion

A balanced diet and a lot of exercise and sport (30 – 60 min/day) are a healthy combination. The right weight furthers well-being and health. Thermals, directional effectiveness, digestive power

There are various criteria for judging the effectiveness of herbs and foodstuffs.

The use of certain herbs and ingredients is based on observations of the effects on the body which these foodstuffs, herbs and spices show after having eaten them. The medical science has developed following system: Every ingredient or herb has a directional effectiveness. Furthermore, there are herbs which have a special effect on certain organs.

The basic condition for a healthy metabolism is to obtain sufficient energy from food and that the digestive process doesn't use too much energy. An easily digestible meal makes content and sated, doesn't cause flatulence and fatigue after the meal. The perfect spices increase the healthiness of our meals. Very often, just small doses of herbs and spices will suffice. They are not used to make us sated, but to help our digestive organs to digest the food.

12.2 Recipes

The recipes list the ingredients to be used and the cooking instructions show how the dish is prepared. The list of ingredients shows the concerned quantities as well as the relevance for the therapy. If you find „less than mentioned", try to comply or find an alternative from the „list of recommended foodstuffs". Mostly it shall result just in a small change of taste when you simply avoid this ingredient.

Mild cooking methods: boiling, stewing, poaching, steaming
Strong cooking methods: barbecuing, roasting, frying, smoking
Balanced cooking methods: deep-frying, baking brick
Deep-freezing and warming in the microwave oven should be avoided (denaturalization).

12.3 Foodstuffs

Foodstuffs have an effect on body and soul like medicinal herbs, only a very much milder one. Dietary advice is mainly based on regional foodstuffs. The knowledge about the effects of each foodstuff and the knowledge, when which foodstuff shall be used, is based on the orthodox school of medicine. Use ecologic-organic products, if possible. As everything should be cooked for a long time due to a better digestability and very rarely eaten raw, the food agrees with everyone.

The classification of the foodstuffs according to their effect on the body is the basis in order to achieve a harmonious status of health.

Dietary advisors do not recommend certain foodstuffs for everyone. The individual diet is tailor-made for the individual constitution.

Buy only fresh and ripe fruit and vegetables. You ought to leave unripe fruit and vegetables and such with brown spots and wilted leaves behind in the market. In this case take deep-frozen goods (never ready-to-serve dishes!). Fruit and vegetables are deep-frozen immediately after harvesting and often contain more vitamins and minerals than the goods from the vegetable shelf. Whereas conserved or tinned goods contain very much less biological substances. Also, salt, sugar and others are mostly added to the latter. Never leave the foodstuffs in the water after washing them to avoid that many vital substances get drowned. Clean salads, fruit and vegetables immediately before serving.

Please make sure of the hygienic processing of foodstuffs. Clean your salads, fruit and vegetables carefully. When cooking with meat, prepare all ingredients first and then process the meat products. Clean the worktop and tools very carefully. Wooden surfaces ought to be treated with a mild disinfectant regularly in order to reduce germination.
Store fruit and vegetables separately, if possible. Harvested fruit and vegetables are still alive and emit e.g. ethylene gas, which makes other products ripen and age faster. Keep meat and fish in the closed packaging or store them in the fridge in closed containers.

12.4 Herbs

There are some basic rules for storing medicinal herbs. On principle, herbs must be protected from direct sunlight, humidity and heat.

Containers for the storage of herbs may be glasses, ceramic jars and even plastic containers. However, plastic is a rather unsuitable material and should only be a short-term solution. In case of glass containers, use a dark material.

Medicinal herbs cannot be kept for any long period. The shelf life of herbs is limited. However, it can be prolonged with suitable storage. The place should be dark, rather cool and absolutely dry. A wooden medicine cabinet, placed not directly next to a source of heat, would be ideal. Never buy large quantities of herbs so as not to have to throw them away. Label the container with the name of the herb and the date of harvesting or processing.

13 Other dietic-books

The following syndromes of dietetics, TCM or for a therapy supplement for cancer are available.

Dietetics

E001. Nutrition of the infant - baby food
E002. Nutrition during lactation
E003. Nutrition in old age
E004. Nutrition of children and adolescents
E005. Nutrition of athletes
E006. Light weight
E007. Pregnancy
E008. Full food

Protein and electrolyte - kidneys

E009. (hemodialysis) dialysis treatment
E010. Acute renal failure
E011. Chronic renal insufficiency
E012. Nephrotic syndrome
E013. Kidney stones (nephrolithiasis)

Gastrointestinal tract - pancreas

E014. Acute pancreatitis (inflammation of the pancreas)
E015. Chronic pancreatitis (inflammation of the pancreas)

Gastrointestinal tract - small intestine and large intestine

E016. Acute obstipation (constipation)
E017. Chronic obstipation (constipation)
E018. Colon irritabile
E019. Diverticulitis
E020. Acquired lactose intolerance (lactose malabsorption)
E021. Fructose malabsorption
E022. Glutensensitive enteropathy (celiac disease)
E023. Colectomy
E024. Short Bowel Syndrome

Gastrointestinal tract - liver, gallbladder, bile ducts

E025. Acute and chronic hepatitis (inflammation of the liver)
E026. Cholelithiasis (bile stones)
E027. fatty liver
E028. cirrhosis

Gastrointestinal tract - Stomach and duodenal intestine

E029. Acute gastritis
E030. Chronic gastritis
E031. Stomach bleeding
E032. Ulcus ventriculi and duodenal ulcer
E033. Condition after gastric surgery

Gastrointestinal tract - oral cavity and esophagus
E034. Stomatitis
E035. Esophageal carcinoma (esophageal cancer)
E036. Refluosophagitis (heartburn)

Special diseases
E037. Phenylketonuria (PKU)
E038. Rheumatic joint diseases

Metabolism
E039. Obesity (overweight)
E040. Diabetes mellitus
E041. Eating disorders (underweight)

Fat metabolism
E042. Hypercholesterolaemia (increased cholesterol level)
E043. Hepatic Encephalopathy

Heart and circulation
E044. Arteriosclerosis (arterial calcification)
E045. Heart insufficiency
E046. Hypertension
E047. Hyperuricaemia and gout

Changed nutrient requirements
E048. In case of fever
E049. For malignant diseases
E050. After burns
E051. Radiation and chemotherapy

CANCER
E100. Pancreatic cancer
E101. Bladder cancer
E102. Blood cancer (leukemia)
E103. Breast cancer
E104. Colorectal cancer
E105. Gastric cancer
E106. Kidney cancer
E107. Esophageal cancer

TCM
E200. Bladder - moisture heat in the bladder
E201. Bladder - moisture and cold in the bladder
E202. Bladder - emptiness and cold in the bladder
E203. Large intestine - external cold affects the large intestine
E204. Large intestine - moisture heat in the large intestine
E205. Large intestine - heat blocks the intestine II acute
E206. Large intestine - dryness of the colon
E207. Large intestine - Yang deficiency (cold)
E208. Heart - Blood insufficiency
E209. Heart - Blood stagnation
E210. Heart - Fire
E211. Heart - Hot mucus clogs the heart pores

E212. Heart - Cold mucus clogs the heart pores
E213. Heart - Qi deficiency
E214. Heart - Yang deficiency
E215. Heart - Yin deficiency
E216. Liver - Ascending Liver Yang
E217. Liver - Blood deficiency
E218. Liver - Blood stagnation
E219. Liver - Moisture heat in liver and gall bladder
E220. Liver - Fire
E221. Liver - Gall bladder Qi-Empty
E222. Liver - Cold in the liver meridian
E223. Liver - Qi stagnation
E224. Liver - Wind
E225. Liver - Wind with ascending liver Yang
E226. Liver - Wind with blood anemic
E227. Liver - Wind with extreme heat
E228. Lung - Qi deficiency
E229. Lung - Mucus-moisture in the lungs
E230. Lung - Mucus-heat in the lungs
E231. Lung - Mucus-cold in the lungs
E232. Lung - Dryness of the lungs
E233. Lung - Wind-heat attacks the lungs
E234. Lung - Wind-cold affects the lungs
E235. Lung - Yin deficiency
E236. Stomach - Bloodstagnation
E237. Stomach - Fire
E238. Stomach - Cold with liquid
E239. Stomach - Nutrition stagnation
E240. Stomach - Qi deficiency
E241. Stomach - Rebellious Qi
E242. Stomach - Yin Emptiness
E243. Spleen - Heat and moisture attack the spleen
E244. Spleen - Coldness and moisture affects the spleen
E245. Spleen - Qi deficiency
E246. Spleen - Qi deficiency + Declining spleen Qi
E247. Spleen - Qi deficiency + spleen does not control the blood
E248. Spleen - Yang deficiency
E249. Kidney - Heart and kidney no longer communicate
E250. Kidney - Jing deficiency
E251. Kidney - Kidneys cannot receive the Qi
E252. Kidney - Qi is not stable
E253. Kidney - Yang deficiency
E254. Kidney - Yin deficiency

For further information visit di-book.com.